O BODY OF BLISS

O BODY OF BLISS

POEMS BY

JANINE CERTO

Longleaf Press - Fayetteville, North Carolina - 2023

Copyright © 2023 by Janine Certo

All rights reserved.

Printed in the United States of America

Cover Art: "In my throat and ribcage, flamenco dancers tap their heels when you approach" by Roger Weingarten

Library of Congress Catalog Data:

Certo, Janine

O Body of Bliss: Poems.

ISBN: 978-1-7343985-4-0 (paperback)

Cover design by Crystal Simone Smith

Book design by Shannon C. Ward

For author inquiries or for information about permission to reproduce selections from this book contact:

Longleaf Press

Fayetteville, North Carolina

Email: longleafpress@gmail.com

ACKNOWLEDGMENTS

I will always be grateful to Roger Weingarten for selecting O BODY OF BLISS for the Longleaf Press Poetry Prize. Roger's brilliant, generous, and loving editorial touch made these poems use language in new ways. I equally thank Kate Fetherston, Shannon Ward and the team at Longleaf Press for selecting my manuscript. I'm indebted to my mentors, especially Dan Albergotti, Vievee Francis and Maria Terrone who had hands in shaping some of these poems. My appreciation to my department chair, Dorinda Carter Andrews, for supporting a sabbatical to give me precious time to write. I thank my writer and artist friends for their encouragement and critical feedback, especially Alecia Beymer, Cyril Caine, Telaina Eriksen, Stephanie Glazier, Sherine Gilmour, Chuck Madansky, Jane Medved, Patty Seyburn, Robin Silbergleid, Marcela Sulak, Sarah Wetzel and James Wyshynski. Gratitude to my partner, John Schaffer, for his love and for being my ideal reader. Lastly, I am grateful for the love and support from my mother, Connie Puntureri, my brother, Jeff, and my dog, Maddox, all of whom I celebrate in these pages.

Grateful acknowledgment to the following journals and editors for publishing these poems, sometimes in slightly different forms or with different titles.

The Cincinnati Review: "My Mother Tells Me She May Have Been the Product of Rape"

The Comstock Review: "O Body of Bliss," "Ways to Heal a Country"

Cream City Review: "Agoraphobia"

The Ilanot Review: "When I Contemplate My Existence"

Italian Americana: "Walking Tour of the Sacred Heart Cemetery," "Prayer for Essential Workers"

Mudfish: "When they took my father's body"

Ovunque Siamo: "Media Lessons in Italian Americana"

Poetry Northwest: "Ode to Hugging"

Red Wheelbarrow: "The Language of Dogs"

Radar Poetry: "On Poets Who Write about Childhood Small-Animal Bludgeoning," "Portrait of Girlhood with Small-Town River and Bar, circa 1981"

Ruminate: "On Buoyancy and the Loss of the Ability to Worry," "In the Winter of My Silence, the Oracle"

Shenandoah: "Breaking My Father Out of the Hospice Unit to Go to the Italian Market," "Saint Michael, the Serpent and the Red Lobster"

SWWIM Every Day: "For Suzanne Valadon Who Painted Nudes

Vallum: "Conspiracy Theory"

Valparaiso Poetry Review: "Elegy for W.S. Merwin"

For my mother, Connie Puntureri

The repose of sleep refreshes only the body...
In the morning we must sweep out the shadows.

—Bachelard

... It is all wrong to imagine paradise
as a state of bliss. It will turn
out to be, in the true spirit of God,
an incessant up and down, a whirlpool
of change.

—Dinesen

TABLE OF CONTENTS

BODY OVER MOUNTAIN

ODE TO HUGGING 1
BREAKING MY FATHER OUT OF THE HOSPICE UNIT TO GO
TO THE ITALIAN MARKET 3
PRAYER FOR ESSENTIAL WORKERS 5
SAINT MICHAEL, THE STEELERS & THE RED LOBSTER 6
ON HEARING THE FORMER ACTING HEAD 8
OF THE CDC SAY, YOU CAN'T GET PEOPLE TO WEAR A
MASK TO PROTECT OTHERS 8
MEDITATION ON THE EVE OF ASH WEDNESDAY 9
ON POETS WHO WRITE ABOUT CHILDHOOD SMALL-
ANIMAL BLUDGEONING 10
THE FUN AUNT'S APARTMENT 12
AGORAPHOBIA 13

BODY AS GROVE AND VINE

WALKING TOUR OF THE SACRED HEART CEMETERY, PINE
TOWNSHIP, PA 17
ELEGY FOR W.S. MERWIN 18
TASTING NOTES 20
MEDIA LESSONS IN ITALIAN AMERICANA 21
THE CAREGIVING WIFE'S CONFESSION 23
PRAYER, COVID, DAY 250 25
CONSPIRACY THEORY 26
CHILDREN AT THE END OF THE WORLD 28
MY BROTHER TELLS ME NO MORE SAD STUFF 30
SELF-PORTRAIT AS A HERMIT IN THE WILD 31

BODY BENEATH WATER AND LIGHT

THE LANGUAGE OF DOGS 35
ORACLE SPEAKS OF RESOLVE 37
ODE TO MY VITO CLARINET 38
FORUM IN WHICH I LOVED YOU 39
ODE TO THE AIRBNB 40
HOW I BECAME A DAUGHTER 41
THE PHOTOGRAPHER 43
REUNION 44

BODY IN SLEEP AND SHADOW

WHEN THEY TOOK MY FATHER'S BODY, THE BAG 47
INSTAGRAM FLOWERS 49
FINAL SCENE OF MINGELLA'S *ENGLISH* 50
SELF-PORTRAIT AS CYPRESS TREES IN A TIME OF GRIEF .. 51
MY MOTHER TELLS ME SHE MAY HAVE BEEN THE PRODUCT OF RAPE 52
FOR SUZANNE VALADON WHO PAINTED NUDES 54
SELF-PORTRAIT AS HOURGLASS 56
ON BUOYANCY AND THE LOSS OF THE ABILITY TO WORRY 57
MY DOG HAD SEIZURES. I KEPT A DIARY 58
I ARGUE WITH MY THERAPIST ABOUT DEFINITIONS 62
ORACLE SPEAKS OF RESILIENCE 63
MEDITATION ON THE GREAT LAKE 65

O BODY OF BLISS

WHEN I CONTEMPLATE MY EXISTENCE 69
SEX 70
PRAYER FOR A STUDENT DRIVER 72
MEDITATION ON A LAVENDER FARM 73
ON READING ESTHER PEREL'S *MATING IN CAPTIVITY* 75
AMONG THE THINGS SHE DOESN'T DESERVE 75
AFTER THE MELT 77

EVENING POEM TO BE READ TO A DOG	79
IN THE WINTER OF MY SILENCE, THE ORACLE	81
WAYS TO HEAL A COUNTRY	82
O BODY OF BLISS	84
NOTES	85

BODY OVER MOUNTAIN

ODE TO HUGGING

It's true as a child I wore a stuffed
bear to emaciation, until her coat
pilled like a favorite sweater. I can
stand to be held at least twenty
seconds, in other words, at this point
in the poem, we'd still be hugging.
Endear me. Cherish me. Hedge me
like a garden. I miss my mother's,
amniotic, her seventy-seven streams
and a faulty valve. Repair me. Mend
me like my friend Sherine with her
trademark lift-off version or my friend
Mary with wet shampooed hair, how
she smells of spiced tea, chocolate.
Oxytocin me. Right-hemispheric-
emotional-process me. My father's
gone, but his Percocet words still
break, *It'll be okay*, a consolation
wobbly as his cane, and I used to find
my brother, now frontline health
worker, open smile, arms perpendicular
as a scarecrow singing my name.
Lower my pressure. Allow me further.
If you're familiar with nature's
reciprocity, I put my arms around
my love, and we are beech trees
grown together, water slow-moving
on the lake. I've been floating. I rest
my chin for the living and how

many of the millions of souls
who could not be together at the end
in these years of no hugging.
I'll meet you. Left-lean you. We're
linked if you catch the imperceptible
shift in a house plant, its long leaves
bent toward the sun and away from
gravity. Every day, we're falling. Hug
as a child would. Who will you greet
in the foyer or through friendship's
revolving door? You could be
tendrils spiraling fingers tight
as a ball point pen spring that if
it could talk would say we're losing
time, this blanket is only so weighted,
and the warm length of the dog is
unpredictable. Stand for the grounded
body human. Touch hunger, touch skin.

BREAKING MY FATHER OUT OF THE HOSPICE UNIT TO GO TO THE ITALIAN MARKET

Even the magnolia was incredulous
at its bloom, glass doors agape
behind us as we rolled him out,
still gowned. Dad's chair barely fit
down an aisle of amaretti,

olives, beans, tomatoes, each pasta
shape its own *regioni*, this small
store crowded and warm, the owner
accommodating with his nods.
We thought we could reach for

peaches or look into a murky
crock of escarole soup or stack
pizzelles and get another
dozen years. We all did it: swabbed
bread cubes in oil and grabbed

that deliciously-stubborn broken
biscotti, working it long in the mouth.
What can I say, except we'd taken
turns in a faded green chair for seven
days, sobs wedged in the solar plexus

as in a vise, my mother on repeat: *These people
have a goal,* my brother knowing the right
drug to keep Dad from becoming
sedated, and me finding the one willing
surgeon. I still feel the aliveness of that

precise moment we changed
our minds, that urgency
to celebrate, an effervescence that comes
from resolve. He died three long years
later. *Forgive me, father. Forgive me, mother.*

What stays with me most was the swerving,
how we navigated Dad over winter's new
cracks, around potholes of East Liberty,
skidded on the gritty spring ash of Pittsburgh,
my brother pushing, my mother to the left,

me to the right,
the masses of bystanders pointing,
laughing, waving as we navigated
a park, a Wendy's parking lot, the GetGo
gas station, workers with their thumbs up

smoking outside the back of a diner, but we
had to stay focused, tried not to look back, and even now
I can't quiet those voices, even now
I still hear them: *Where do you think they're headed?*
What are they doing? What the hell are they doing?

PRAYER FOR ESSENTIAL WORKERS

Bless the beginning, elemental, fundamental. Before all
others in order. Rising early. Bless the pills dispensed
from a drive-through transaction door like a tongue.
Bless enough PPE. Bless the nurse, the nightingale,
born from *night* and the Old English *galan*, known
to carol over the grind of cities' background noise.
Bless the manufacturer, the firefighter, the ventilated,
the sought and rescued, the salvaged, mopped up
and overhauled. Bless the teacher who resets the history
button. Bless the shift with an officer who deescalates.
Bless the liquor store and bottle. Bless the grocer and their
continual stream of conveyor belt like fresh-paved asphalt
and what it is to do a thing mindfully and skillfully. Bless
the covered and the wrapped. Somebody is weary or sick,
and a miraculous bag of soup with a roll is delivered
on their stoop. Bless the driver, the soaring, open
leaves of the door. Bless the answer, the acknowledgment,
the coming back. Bless the park-loop walking route
and the mail carrier. Give them a Bill of Rights, for they've all
been looking for a good morning, afternoon or night, like
that delivery person whose name on your phone was Grace.

SAINT MICHAEL, THE STEELERS & THE RED LOBSTER

Women should not adorn the body with ornaments, Peter says,
but in the mid-80s, every Madonna bangle & hoop was a tunnel
out of Western PA. I could've piked & dove; ducked, tucked
& rolled through their glint. Timothy cautions to exercise

the womanly body profiteth little; only godliness is profitable.
I felt God running the mile in school. Only a few girls on the team
had that kind of endurance. Corinthians says women must remain
silent in churches. I never said *Jesus Christ* watching The Steelers,

but I curled the phrase *the Lord's name in vain*, tongued the slant
rhyme of it, how it sounded like sin, something worthy
of a box with a priest hoarding my sins as if stacking crisp
ones. I tell you, the best part of Saturday Mass

was after Saturday Mass: *Red Lobster*© with its red carpet, hush-
puppies, Ultimate Feast & the trinity of my parents & brother:
my father, muse of suffering; the son he was harder on; my
mother, proclaimed survivor, each distinct, but a single

essence, all stylin' & dressed up after a day weeding the hill.
I performed the sitting, standing, kneeling & though filled
in the baptism of our above-ground pool, though filled
with thanks like the last stanza of a closing hymn,

my brother & I couldn't stop staring at this one stained-
glass window. What have I taken? A love that makes my knees
buckle. In the background, a landscape of mountains, a small
town. In the foreground, Saint Michael about to slay the green
dragon under a sandal, every organ chord: *not here, not this town, this
creed*. We sat in a pew in the back. My mother let me sit on the end.

PORTRAIT OF GIRLHOOD WITH SMALL-TOWN RIVER AND BAR, CIRCA 1981

Who wasn't shoved in a room by Boy Who Would Grow Up
to Be Rapist, his hands at work while her friends picked the lock?
Who would be saved one night after a van sputtering Moonglow
stopped, and a man chased the girls through backyards,
pinned one cold to the ground until she kicked, then ran a run
she still dreams of, feet weighted like barbell discs? I tell you,
we stayed in groups, passed the gym, door propped to the sweat
smell of rubber, past older boys breaking outside the pizzeria,
Billy Squier stroking the transistor behind the counter. We crossed
the lot of *Small-Town River and Bar,* door ajar to the smoke
strange dark in summer, men gesturing with their bottles to come.
All we wanted were Zero bars, Mars bars, and those waxed lips
we'd toss after the gag was over, or, if we were lucky, go on
that Paris trip in high school after what parents called the fleeting
years of finger jello, jimmied cake, and truth or dare in basements when
parents let children sleep out on the porch where Johnny,
uninvited to the glider, slid a soiled thumb down the blade of a hunting
knife. What it was like: they grabbed us on roadsides, their chests
like hounds out a Chevy, hands sweeping our behinds. They grabbed
us bolting lawns skirted with azaleas, down tight halls between periods,
beneath the tracks by the river, as if they were pulled aside, taught to gaze
past a body like their mother's. No one knew but the bright crown
vetch along the bank, the coal piles' lesser mountains, and the split
level homes with garages open like dirty mouths threatening to eat us.

ON HEARING THE FORMER ACTING HEAD OF THE CDC SAY, YOU CAN'T GET PEOPLE TO WEAR A MASK TO PROTECT OTHERS

I think of those older kids who crushed
fireflies between their thumbs and fingers, then

smeared the jeweled kill on others' ears.
At nine, I knew nothing of enzymes, but knew

why dandelions closed, that waves
of fenceless yards lent a peculiar sense of being

airborne. Isn't the soft-bodied beetle like Truth,
a surrender, bioluminescent? Easy, I suppose,

what couldn't be seen. I chased their laughing
train as it darted the night, broke and looped,

the stars and stripes the sound of screaming.

MEDITATION ON THE EVE OF ASH WEDNESDAY

Was this the dust from which God
fashioned girls: a *Sports Illustrated*

issue with a model thumbing
the sand? At the end of holy month,

our due feast: bird, ham, starch, lamb,
melt-away eggs, molds of white

and dark chocolate chicks
and crosses. Our mothers

spooned us a religion
of grapefruit, tuna, crisp celery

stalks like pale dress pants,
confirming our appetites binge

lent binge years of penance
and prayer to unlearn, to fill

our baskets green, to bite just
one square of a bar, to stop

at a slice of meringue pie with
its beading skin. Isn't it violent

what we do to the rabbits? Heads.
Then bodies.

ON POETS WHO WRITE ABOUT CHILDHOOD SMALL-ANIMAL BLUDGEONING

There is a grassy kindness to what
soaks in the plump shade before

its unfortunate spotting, before
hands ram sticks—preadolescent

gods hammering their crossroad signs
into the ground. You own the brown

liver, lungs, guts, blood—a kaleidoscope
like a mother's emptied

purse. You didn't have to take
the coach's command in the huddle,

the others pumping one another up.
Back then, a cheer was the stirring

chirp of Descartes's animal-machine
theory, but now through the pane

of your mind's eye, you alter stone-
flower-stone around your dead thing,

anticipating the reader stitching threads
of compassion because someone

bigger just split, left you crushed—or
worse, charged at you. I've known men

who take ice picks to add notches to their
belts, men who think nothing of chasing

any body through a dark wood or down
a sun-lit path, so you may be surprised

to learn that I see your gesture as earnest
with the turn to the soft landing, your exquisite
heart the shape of a Spike-thumb Frog.

THE FUN AUNT'S APARTMENT

—for Dolly Flowers

I learned to swear on Sundays, shuffled cards
at the Formica: *Aces Wild, Spit in the Ocean, Follow
the Queen, Oh, Shit!* Stacks of pennies, lined-up
liquors, Ritz crackers, cheeseballs, bowls of Brach's,
vintage perfumes on the dresser, gossip magazines
strewn in a basket she bought in Panama, travel
magnets littering the outside of her fridge, twenty-
six crocheted pillows on the bed, photos of men
displayed like museum artifacts in her cabinet.
She collected 106 salt & pepper shakers, let us
choose one to take. She let us eat: Klondikes, Pringles,
orange chews, frozen Snickers. Even her name meant
abundance. Her velvet curtains done so well,
they framed the window like you could reach
in & touch that gleaming green bottle of wine, the pear
turned yellow from the sun. She wanted me to take
my favorite set. I took the floral ones, the pepper top
rusted black. When they took her leg, I bet the blood
ran fucking gorgeous like opened petals to a Chinese
fan. She made everything salted, spicy, sugared & fine.
Her apartment: 700 square feet. A freezer full
of things we weren't permitted.

AGORAPHOBIA

On my knees before the first leaves to open—
—Jennifer Militello

you're reminded of walking
paths picking strawberries,

dogwoods scattering their white,
how all that outside waits,

some winged thing between
window & screen & for no

reason, ground swell: extraction
of air, a geodesy flipped like

hands slipping off the Earth
or missing the exit & caught

in a line of cars, semis, a hundred
moths colliding in your chest

& the heart's misfiring, then
over a bridge then catapulting

through a tunnel, the dark
an interminable river & someone

keeps mouthing *Bend*
backwards over this mountain.

BODY AS GROVE AND VINE

WALKING TOUR OF THE SACRED HEART CEMETERY, PINE TOWNSHIP, PA

For my great grandparents, Saverio and Josephine

Smoke in my pores, ashes on my tongue,
I tell the guide you died at the face of a coal pillar, ten
years after you immigrated from Calabria. You
are the only clear face on a headstone. I tell

the guide you died at the face of a coal pillar
among the split and broken, sinking and crumbling.
You're the only clear face on a headstone. I study
your ceramic black-white photo: dark hair

among the split and broken, sinking and crumbling.
Your wife wore mourning clothes the rest of her life.
I study your ceramic black-white photo: dark hair
waving like my grandparents, my father. Your

wife wore mourning clothes the rest of her life
trying to find a ghost who lived in a boarding house.
Waving like my grandparents, my father, I traveled
one summer for a granita in your birth town, trying

to find a ghost who lived in a boarding house. I
imagined you there, a young man holding your son. I
traveled one summer for a granita in your birth town,
smoke in my pores, ashes on my tongue.

ELEGY FOR W.S. MERWIN

—When the time comes, I will follow the black dog.

That day, my dim office turned
cold as if someone left
the shutters gaping. Firetails
retreated to their favorite
roosting places. The one

bat hung from the eaves
like a pendant light. Later,
strange quietude, the clouded
night tipping
its hat. A falcon seized
a pigeon whose body

twisted to petals, jadeite,
opened to a silk Vietnamese
fan. It was like the end
of the year, dark and wind
at their peak—everything
punctuated by nothing,

save swirling translations
of rage and love, love
and despair. Over nature's
carols, odes, roundels,
and ballads, I rose to find
lines: *meadow, the other side,*

and hoped he was right.
Stones crowded river
beds like human greed.
No, it was grief.

Somewhere, a man takes
a solitary walk

after garden work. There
is wood smoke, birdsong,
a pineapple pulled from a grove—
the jacket opened, a forest
of waxed palms continuing
to grow, a music

reverberating like leaves
falling or rain, an utterance
like a million monarchs released
for the migration or an open
book imploding.

TASTING NOTES

Raspberry, lush cherry color, and on the nose, cedar
laced with thyme, cocoa powder, pencil tips, and grass
blades like ones between teeth of children pleading

to pick from the trellis, their feet scrubbed clean until
they burned. Bold like anarchists, strangers to terroir
and body, they marched, sang, crushed between toes

an elixir yielding a core of smoke and olive, complex
and intense. They couldn't appreciate yet
how it was best served with aged cheeses, rich

sauces, pastas, two-foot long and hollow, but they stole
perciatelli from their parents' cellar, dipped their straws
in the barrel, sipped it up, pretended it blood.

MEDIA LESSONS IN ITALIAN AMERICANA

Break off a cheese so brittle
it flakes like paint from a fresco,
then rattle your Campari on ice.
Dip bread in anything that flows
like water, glistens like oil, gels
and coagulates like stew. Be loyal
as the length of a hound's back,
generous as lemons gifting
from a tree. Hide behind your humor
as beef nestles in cabbage. Go big
as a sandwich or hair or a full
mouth. Get the sordid details
of a death, then drag out
the biscotti jar like an urn. Stand
by a pot cooking sauce. Sit,
kneel. At the restaurant, bitch
about the tough calamari. Don't
come in the door unless you got
the sopressatta. You'll have to answer
for it if the provolone's soft; you're dead
if it's too salty. Check on the tomatoes
in the garden every hour. Turn
everything gold like batter
in a pizzelle iron. Create, create,
procreate, but don't let newborns
in public until they're baptized, lest
they become victim to the evil eye,
and when you die, a gondolier

bellowing Pavarotti will row you to
Aunt Mary, Uncle Tony,
& the blessed Virgin taking you
into her bosom and holding tongs
that twirl you a third nest of pasta.
But you won't see your cousin Vic,
that motherfucker, who gave a lousy
five bucks at the wedding of your daughter.
Be as blue as the blue in a Bernini
fountain, as anxious as a narrowing
coastline road winding, all
those scooters, buses
honking. Hold onto principles
like castelvetrano olives hold onto their skin,
like houses cling to a cliff by the sea.
When night comes, pick from a carcass,
layer meat, more cheese, basil on a roll,
down the last of the Chianti, then drop
into the deepest sleep.

THE CAREGIVING WIFE'S CONFESSION

She told me they thought about it, how
easy it would be to go down to the garage,

turn the ignition on, how they'd do it
at lunchtime, but I can't

remember why because I'd checked
out, like precipitous leakage

in the lung vessels, like that
flashback cinematic technique

where a character imagines herself
and her partner from the chest

up in the front seat of a car riding over
a bridge, the top down, stereo piping

through the tunnel. They've thrown
their heads back a last time, their

scarves perfumed with notes
of vanilla or almond,

the man neat and slick in tinted
shades, button down

shirt, cuffs rolled up—
the one he wore in Florida or to

visit children as part of a road trip,
the woman touching up her lipstick

in the passenger seat mirror, no
exhaust today, just pressing on.

PRAYER, COVID, DAY 250

I dropped
an entire box
of toothpicks,
the carnage
across the tiled
continent
of my floor.
In the city
my ancestors
landed, I think,
how many others
have fallen to their
hands & knees?

CONSPIRACY THEORY

a circle of reason / a proof that cannot
be proved or disproved / a mad mixture /

a template for order / cast, shaped, ready-
made and launched / requires immediate

response (response must have no minor
errors) / a distrust / a witch hunt /

an elaborate dance / behind the scenes /
eyewitness testimony / no discussion

of shortcomings / a lying song /
a hunch gone wrong / the plunge

of an economy / the rise of a demagogue /
lurking, scheming, webbing / it spreads

like famine / birthed from drought /
it's birther and denier / the death

of science / a plot / a hoax / a code /
a cover-up / knee-jerk / whatever

works / it spawns movements / the uncited /
the alt-right / a need served / epistemic,

existential, self-defeating / off the cliff /
a riff / an election rigged / the rewritten,

staged and misplaced / the towers that never
fell / a genocide erased / the Evil Incarnate /

the Machiavellian-slick / the mouse's click /
a spiral into alienation and anomie /

a sense-making in a world otherwise
confusing / otherwise good people.

CHILDREN AT THE END OF THE WORLD

The boy on Wildwood kneels
to tap my dog, Maddox, on the crown,
lifts his right then left paw with a dignity
becoming of a knighting ritual. Quarantined,
we exchanged letters— ones we sealed,

marched down the street. He called
himself Laserboy, emitting beams
to fight for justice. I'm drawn
to kids like him who care children
are separated at the border

like zoo cubs; kids who pen a wide-ruled
manifesto to our President to call him
mean. In red caps, unmasked,
white supremacists slung rifles;
plotted to attack the State Capitol;

kidnap the Governor, while an eight-
year-old designed a Black Lives Matter
sign. The president said nothing,
opened a steakhouse menu, rolled
back environmental regulations,

while a boy opened the wings of trifold
like the lungs of planet. He animated
a science project, knew how to protect
shrimp from losing their eyes, that owls
can make a three-quarters revolution
with their heads. Bowed, I can't keep

children from the devastating
blaze of hundreds of thousands
of fallen leaves. I feel the swell
of grief: the five-year-old

in Detroit, Skylar Herbert, first
Michigan child who died of covid,
daughter of EMTs, smile with a lost
tooth in front, "a girl,"
her mother said, "who would run over

and hug you." All through the pandemic,
the boy halted from me as he should.
He remembered the name Maddox
meant *good* & *true*. A letter arrived
from the near-humanless

outside, & this is what
I leaned into, what I still
lean into: a child across the street
meandered like a delta,
knew the answer to every question

was as unpolluted as a sky
under which he'd finished
Zooming, heading out to meet
with a pod like all the others
scattered like photons. When
it rains, the youth don't break.

MY BROTHER TELLS ME NO MORE SAD STUFF

Sometimes, I'd rather be down
south where conch sleep, heavy
organs, but then again, hands might
wake me to sit glossy on a shelf.
When I was young, I collected
ceramic dolls, one for each birthday.
I loved one not more than the other.
I have no idea where they are now.
Once, in performance art, an emperor
imperceptibly ascended a stairwell
to ambient music, taking the entire
length of the show, a cape trailing velvet.
At the top, he placed a dead mouse
in a bird's nest, surrounded it with shards
of flowers. Today, I wrote by a window
framed with squirrels. I made eggs
at supper. Don't worry, brother,
some of the saddest things are beautiful,
and the sky today the palest blue.

SELF-PORTRAIT AS A HERMIT IN THE WILD

In a pandemic, I am keeper of a dog and a garden,
the yews and the cherry hedge. I grow myself
zucchini, arugula and radish below a bamboo
trellis, this urge to redeem the world through

simplicity: a breakfast of greens, Himalayan
salt, one egg. I go into town when I run out
of food. Dawn mouths her odd silence. A heron
cruises low as I walk. Its orange legs sliver air

like silk. A deer stopped, full-faced, a kindness
in this stoic road. I learn the scholarship
of squirrels' patterns, wisps of gray-black above
my husband's ears, my dog's pupils as I clip his

dewclaws to a safe length. If I expect a visitor,
I sweep the path to the gate. I weed, pull thought
into non-thought. I scrub dirt daily from floors.
Nights pass, rain: poplar and pine, willow

and branching palm. I found a finch stunned
on the neighbor's driveway, left talon twitching
its fear. I boxed it, holes and bowl and bit
of seed, placed it in my open garage and waited.

From the kitchen, where I'd thought of suffering, death
all these days, I saw it perch on the box's edge, bend
to drink before whirring away. Some days, I float.
Disembodied. I want to know each name so I can

chant them. Call others to circle. None of this
myth, none of this God, but a bird so big
it climbs 90,000 miles before it has room to turn.
There are other earths and heavens than these.

I retreat to my cave thinking of those who have died
who are so deep in the clouds I know
not where, who were, too, in love with everything.

BODY BENEATH WATER AND LIGHT

THE LANGUAGE OF DOGS

Lab Mix. Found without tags. Same
black coat, same weight, same name

as my dead dog of two days. I paced
outside the cages. An eleven-year-old

beagle shot me a look of disappointment,
then turned her back to me. The vet said

they do that sometimes, become grief-
stricken of never being chosen. The dog

I came for had visible ribs, a patchy fur,
lost from stress. The volunteer escorted

us to a private room. I already knew
I was good at this, armed with training

treats for when he sat, shook. I took him for
a test walk. He pulled, zigzagged the trees,

our route circuitous. I drove off with Harley,
a temporary leash, and a bag of dogfood.

He slept in the relief of the backseat, in the balm
of my satisfaction, strangely like driving

a loved one home from the hospital, held on
all sides by blue and the branched silences

and hesitation of Thelonious Monk.
Home, he played limply with a toy, fed

from the old dog's bowl, slept in the new bed.
But when he woke, he leaped on the couch

and upon catching his reflection in a mirror, broke
a lamp. Stunned, confused, he barked without stop,

watched and waited for what I would do. What
he would do. There, in the clash of sporadic

sun and oak, he towered, back legs rooted, almost
eye-level with me, chest forward as if on display, a face

of love howling, a face so right to be asking:
Now what?

ORACLE SPEAKS OF RESOLVE

Why   keep

scaring yourself? Well,

if   that's what

you're really after, you

                will.

ODE TO MY VITO CLARINET

You were the turf, the loyal marcher, the topped dog, the cold
bleachers, a gift from my parents to keep me from cheerleading.
You advanced me to first chair, taught me cruelty: when Mr. Shira

left 8th period, he returned to a mob of stands raised fully. O, beggar
of embouchure, pepper mill of parade, fourth obelisk of the orchestra,
once a fine segmented specimen, you're now severed under the bed

in five pieces & cased. Forgive that period you were a lamp base. O,
ligature of youth, you were my thumb rest & reed, my barrel, joint
& bell. Didn't I swab you to dry out your bore? O, uncool sister

to the sax, I wasn't Goodman or Shaw, but for thirty minutes, three times
a week, my revenge on the edge of the bed. O, bridge key & ring, I kissed
you behind the door, playing *The Way We Were* again and again and again.

FORUM IN WHICH I LOVED YOU

Of course it was better there
with Lake Como in the speedboat
wake, froth like crema
that clung to the top
of the Legnone in the distance
which I found myself tracing
like the lip of an Americano
I had in Milan. Somewhere
in Leicester, someone hoped
for more than a bland fish
mimicking a Michelangelo
sculpture with its wide eye
clouded over. After a shower,
you leaned into Siena's light,
perfumed as bergamot,
and a peacock in the villa
courtyard of Pope Julius II
shook his feathers twenty-
five times per second before
iridescence. We took Amalfi's
hairpin coastal drive twisting
like the plot of a libretto. I showed
you Scilla's beach of stones and all
the Calabrian villages. We found
the forno with that biscotti
we loved. Before it fell to ruin,
we scooped and sampled,
waded, glided in the shallows
near Venice's watery palm.

ODE TO THE AIRBNB

I'm exhilarated when a host gives me
a good review: the flat in Austin, a hut
in the woods, a cabin on a farm, the sheep
wagon in Joshua Tree, an Airstream
in Wyoming. I've never done the canal
boat or the geodesic dome, and I don't own
a TV like God's breakfast tray, a Nori basket
stockpiled with menus, or owl planters birthing
succulents on the sill. But I'll take a wrapped
candy from a child's painted cup. In the kitchen,
EAT and Live, Laugh, Love
signs I'd never hang seem to work,
as do fairy lights and this complimentary
wine I pour. Ah, the glory and habit breaker
of other people's dish towels, sugar bowls, pen
holders, forks and coffee grinders, their book
shelves and banana hangers. If the house is
in the body and the room is in us, isn't it
sacred to be someone else, stepping over
the threshold into their skin, into the history
of closets, into the wall spaces between framed
photos, bound in their hall light, their wanderings
and absences, their quilts and smells, the lives
of the hearth and the lock on the storage room?
How strange this sun setting on the opposite
side from mine. Two beds, one bath, pets considered,
wifi, and free parking in a town I could never
afford, one with that bistro I'll book for sure,
one the owners frequent where I picture them happy.

HOW I BECAME A DAUGHTER

I stood, slid a foot into a pale
sock, assumed I was born
for a bedroom at the end

of a hallway, a bedroom
with a mirrored closet flooded
with light. I listened, begged

not to eat flesh, buried it in my plate.
Barefoot, I unspooled the yards
as if they were mine. They gave me

jewel boxes and dolls; my brother watches
and keys. I yearned to stay out later.
I stepped into dreams like cotton

gowns, studied a swirled ceiling, recited
catalogues of prayers, commenced
the obsession: my death, the death

of my parents, my brother, every
pet caged and countered or leashed
and left on the patio slab. When the men

came I was told, *Stay inside*. When
the boys came, I was told, *Lock
the doors*. I was made to think the lamb

was me. I cut through fields and fell
in love, crossed my legs, pulled my shoulders
back, broke into a skip the whole way

home. I found myself
wedged between two hands.
I found my forced smile,

my foundation on stilts.
My father told me of trees, the oak
posing, all curves. I longed to be

the woman who named me. Staring
out the window washing dishes,
she said, *Go on, get out of the house. Go on now.*

THE PHOTOGRAPHER

You pick up your camera and become the hawk sensing
the rising of thermal air, trying to capture whatever he's
hunting. You are written with light, your process elusive
as vapor. You take pictures from this height with a hum
that thrills like the woods. In my expression, you find
the sliding board from my childhood, how I find kindness
in a buttoned-down shirt and a butterfly crossing my path.
Such violent clinging, taking a thing inside cells,
holding the other in a landscape where we are born
to lose one another anyway. The photograph's a blanket
spread across one dream into the next among the art
of dying trees. This is the never again. The never enough
to drink, the turn to memory to search the architecture
of a face. It was remarkable how the light changed.

REUNION

Grove City Park, PA, 1980-1983

Wagons descend like green-backed
herons crooning *Crazy Little Thing*

Called Love: a pasta salad, the six
layer jello side like a fourth

cousin your uncle's new
girlfriend brings. The sun, bronzed

like a commemorative coin, shines
off a grill firing up its drum

of stories, the oldest
aunt shouldering the yoke. Isn't

each deviled egg a construction? Each
lift of aluminum foil a *hush-hush?* Canoes

line the shore like cantaloupe
wedges. You can't leave, the adults say,

until you've visited the newborn stretched
on a quilt in the grass. Memories are like

soda bottles, squeezing in, the Polaroid snap,
and how I'd leave it for the boy returning

to lifeguard, how I'd leave it all to lie back.

BODY IN SLEEP AND SHADOW

WHEN THEY TOOK MY FATHER'S BODY, THE BAG

they slid him in was covered with lint and dust. He would have hated
that. He used to point and gently say, *Pick*

that up for me, please; or, I'd spot the top of his head, grooming
the carpeted steps on his way up. When they took my father's body,

they zipped him like a jacket—gone the beautiful
and quiet, the tightness

of anticipatory grief in my chest, and the fear
my mother's atrial fibrillation would trip. When

they took my father's body,
an hour before, I'd been asleep in the next room. Still

alive, the ventilator screaming, Brother in another room,
Mom on the couch, finally asleep after tending

to him through the night. My brother found him
first, came to get us with just a nod. Before they took my father's

body, we consecrated salt and water; recited a prayer for the dead.
What he would have wanted. They took

my father's body. I wasn't prepared for how fast.
We stood back, and I don't know why my first

thought was that I needed to know
how tall the trees had grown that he planted years ago

outside Saint Michael's Church, how he folded a palm
into a cross, how he touched up those scratches on my two-

door coupe, how he never yelled when I almost burned
down the house, that I never said thank you

for going and never told him I'm sorry
I couldn't find that chicory at Giant Eagle he'd asked for twice

that week. When they lifted my father's body, he was the weight
of business: the director from Jefferson Memorial and two mute

blue suits. The clinical feel I hated. When they took his
body, it was a Saturday. They said, *I'm sorry for*. . .when they took

my father's body, I followed them out, pulling off the lint and dust.

INSTAGRAM FLOWERS

Everyone seems to snap more flowers: the crocus
style luring hungry
bees, myrtle defending soil from weeds.

A lens pulled back, denial; up close, a lover,
such communal rehearsal of light and obscurity.
Who's to blame for the failed or flowered?

Can't any bird in a frame be Satan or sower?
In my feed, this world's more heavenly.
We graduate dandelions from weeds. Aren't we

botanists, takers, borrowers—no
different from hawk or backyard bunny? After
supper, I walk the quiet colognes of flowers,

while a neighbor jerks the latch on his mower,
and a cardinal drops her undigested seeds.
I like to snap the short-lived flowers;

I stop for the grape hyacinth, bend and cower.
Back home, I filter a tulip. A Lily of the Valley.
I amp up the yellow in my Wordsworth flower.
I have to believe what dies returns, variously.

FINAL SCENE OF MINGELLA'S *ENGLISH*

Patient. Always my dilemma, my longing
like catching a ride on the back of a truck,
my longing an abbey or bell tower; a cave
or wall of cypress, each one a possible
lover, one cloud hovering like a compassionate
nurse. It's the goddamn endings that get me,
not just the Val d'Orcia cloaked in loss, but the
coming to the end of a perfect work. Such
a rush of completion! Characters leaving, carrying
with them their own stories. Or maybe I'm just
missing Italy, clinging as I do to sunlight
and hope. What I'm saying is Minghella's
dead, and sometimes doesn't this world just
disappoint? But never a plane
in the sky. I want astonishment in the shape
of a Renaissance garden, the arc of Herodotus,
or fully formed shells near the delta. My
god, all this desert once under the sea.

SELF-PORTRAIT AS CYPRESS TREES IN A TIME OF GRIEF

It's not because they're known as drama trees,
all six of them lit, fragrant, garlanded.

You don't normally bend with every breeze,
but serve others with purpose: wood for doors

of Roman Basilicas, stalwart ships,
the harpsicord. If the evergreens stand

for the symbol of glory— candle-shaped
as immortal souls, then they, too, must stand

for grief. Who hasn't been Cyparissus—
Apollo's banishing them to branch,

tears for sap, fastigated to the sky,
felled after being pruned too far?

MY MOTHER TELLS ME SHE MAY HAVE BEEN THE PRODUCT OF RAPE

She says it turns out mice have chewed
around the one tree outside her apartment,
and now the tree will have difficultly drinking.
The landscaper called it *girdling*. I shudder,

thinking this could explain why
my grandmother never hugged
my mother. She says mice are pretty sneaky
and tend to feed on bark by burrowing

above-ground beneath the snow,
which makes me think how my grandmother
shook imperceptibly anytime she was startled.
My mother says she tried to find

the answer herself. She says that as we speak,
they're likely moving from tunnel to tree,
and in May, the damage will affect the leaves.
I want to cry, this snowfall

a scatter-hush outside; the bastard
oak embraces the sky, and my mother
on the couch returns to solitaire
on her phone. There is no answer,

except the past with its muffled timbre,
and my grandmother always sweeping

snow off her hedges, wiping
off counters, cabinets and my questions never

got anywhere and my own shame
gnaws at me now for taking
from the dark cakes my grandmother made,
yet never getting why she took

pills with a bottle of rubbing alcohol after
she withdrew one spring. If only I
could be an arborist, give my mother a sight
more solid than silence. I can only remember that
tree is derived from the same root as *true*.

FOR SUZANNE VALADON WHO PAINTED NUDES

    Dance at Bougival, Pierre-Auguste Renoir
    1882-1883

In this painting of summer smolder,
a chap in cap, workman shirt blue,

is leading, spinning you, a woman
with a white petticoat fume. They tried

to lock you in the eighteenth century. Your subject
previously relegated only to men,

your curved eyebrows like brush
strokes, the lines you blazed in history:

    a woman, fulsome, leg out over the edge
    of a bathtub;

    a woman, reclining, securing
    her hat;

    a woman, standing, feet spread
    firmly with a hand mirror;

    a woman, foot on a stool, preparing
    for a wash.

What irony within this frame, you
hidden under a red bonnet. Were you

wondering if women could ever win? After Warren,
I wondered it, too. Just yesterday,

my neighbor, the Drain Commissioner, rolled
in from out of town, barefoot

and shirtless, scotch
in hand, and crossed our street, fireworks

exploding, to tell me: *I hear you paint
nudes. I paint nudes. I'm actually a nudist. Do*

you want to show each other our nudes?

SELF-PORTRAIT AS HOURGLASS

~ say logic ~ say particulate matter ~ obsession

with the character of the cessation of something ~

a break from labor ~ a marker ~ a bronze-

gilt ~ a specific height and diameter ~

~ say travel ~ say mind ~ a stream

of thoughts ~ a want for wings ~

predecessor of the clepsydra ~

dating back to the times of Babylon ~

~say vessel~ say ship ~ stop it quick— throw

back glass ~ fists of sand ~ a SLOW sign

construction site ~ hold your breath ~ calibrated ~

~ fine-tuned ~ thwart these little ~

deaths

ON BUOYANCY AND THE LOSS OF THE ABILITY TO WORRY

The eye of a crocodile self-adjusts, swims
its sinusoidal pattern a hundred miles across
the sea to feed on turtles, how worry comes

from the word *wyrgan*, to seize by the throat
& tear. When peonies burst, it reminds
me there's nothing to hold onto. I like my

cinnamon scone with coffee in a porcelain
cup. I like to practice holding the small, light
& cheerful. I rake & listen to the neighbor's

kid teach me how lemurs have padding on
their feet so they stick if they have to jump,
& how a family bonds. Lately, every sound

I trace is my dead father's voice: *Don't!*
Or is it: *Don't let anything pass you by*? Here's
to the shifting mantle of sky, the *schliff* of my

book's turning pages, attending this ten
vegetable soup I've made myself with
its cornucopia of colors, everything cut

down to size, & what
can't be known in my dog's
whimpering dream. He's swimming.

MY DOG HAD SEIZURES. I KEPT A DIARY.

We'd done everything: right vet, right backup
service, right tests, right meds, raced frantic
as ER nurses at that blood-curdling screech,
talked him through the swim, dabbed saliva
and urine from his dark coat, fetched
the mop from the basement. First seizure:
March 26, 2012, 5:00am. Length: one
minute with nine-minute postictal state. He fell
down a flight of steps. Barking, significant
stumbling, blindness. Possible causes:
busy time at work for me or the shift
to spring. Put up gate by steps. October 13,
4:15pm. Fifteen-second aura followed by thirty-
second seizure and one

minute postictal state. His
expression turned frozen
staring out the window from his chair.
He seemed to smell something which triggered
whimpering. Froth at the face.
Possible cause: change again in the weather. Begin
Phenobarbital. This went on another year: 2:30
am, 8:30pm, 1:00am, like an anxious
human pacing in a storm. Was it the oil paints?
The new cedar fence? New toothpaste? That green
apple slice? Did he go to bed too late?
I noted not to put him through periods of exertion.
October 29, 2013, 5:30pm. *Cluster* seizure,

characterized by seizures one after another, unresolved
can result in death. Action: give Diazepam for seizures

lasting more than five minutes or for cluster seizures.
Eliminate all toxins. Alternate high quality sources
of protein. Give filtered water. Engage in stimulating
yet nonstressful play sessions. Be vigilante about evening
snack for blood sugar levels. Don't go out to dinner.
Keep environment predictable. But when my father was declining
and my mother was exhausted and my husband, too, left
because his father was dying, I prayed. It was the first
terrible thing I did. June 17, 2014,
4:30pm. When my friend called to say, "He's
gone," I was sure she meant broke loose from his collar.
"I'd just returned from the grocery,"
she said, "and his head was resting on his paws."
My lungs dropped like soaked sponges, then the second

terrible thing I did, I made her get a second
opinion to confirm. A neighbor's voice, "Yes,"
then my friend back on crying. The third terrible
thing I did was ask if she gave Harley his pills.
Of course she did. I hung up, collapsed
on my parents' carpet, then stood into a sob,
a writhe and cadence of Nothing-Is-Ours, not
even the crumb of sky under which I lost
my grip on a balloon as kid, and as it rose, I was filled
with a terror of what pressure can do. My dog was a Black
Retriever without a tail. People said he resembled a bear.
When we ran, he buried his muzzle in the waves

of snow, leaped the cold mounds as a dolphin leaps wave
after wave. He waited for his feet to be wiped,
fussed, pawed, and barked at his bed, rotating
his body. He adjusted that bed until it was
to his liking. He clung low in grass to appear slight
in front of children and other dogs and animals. He rested
his head on his toys, stole our socks, paper
balls from our baskets, pausing in the hallway light
to taunt us. He was three when he died. I'm sorry,
my friend who watched him, I never said,
"How awful for you." I couldn't
talk about it for years. When
you tried, I changed the subject. Thanks for calling
your boyfriend, for wrapping Harley in that lavender
blanket. Thanks for driving

his body to the clinic until I drove
back home. I'm sorry, Husband,
I wasn't there in Virginia. I'm sorry, Father-in-law.
I wasn't with you in hospice. Sorry,
my dog. Sorry I wasn't
there. Alone,
confused, you
must have expected me. I've imagined my own
death by bear. I think I'd be alright with
that one-after-another tear, the bear
up on his hind legs, last embrace
before knocking me down, taking a bite
or two of my arm then seizing a leg before being
dragged into his woods. Because I'm
haunted. I didn't
come as you cluster seized when you must

have known you were going to a place of no stairs, no
corners, no leashes, just a dropped
stick, rot vibrating the Earth, the air's bloom
of grass and soil, then running straight for
the ocean— and how fast your legs paddled
waves that
kept on coming, sea foam like snow clustering
all around you, and for a second
you believed it might
not happen, but with every terrible
minute passing, you were being dragged
by a wolf pack that gave
rise to you with the hunter
orange sun just fading, and you never came back.

I ARGUE WITH MY THERAPIST ABOUT DEFINITIONS

Bare branches in winter sometimes resemble
nerves, but that doesn't mean hysteria.

It could just be the wind. My Authentic Happiness-
Beautiful Day ends by letting my dog gnaw the last

third of an apple as I hold the dwindling core
with my index finger pointer. No matter

how long it takes. I trace the shapes of ghosts.
You tell me to notice is to notice that a W is two V's

that looks like a butterfly. What did I do this morning?
To stave off shame, waiting for water to boil, I revived

an aloe stem, sharp and darkening, then a friend called
to tell me that her chicken

looks her straight in the eye.

ORACLE SPEAKS OF RESILIENCE

> Brazilian Family Finds Red-Footed
> Tortoise, Gone Missing Since 1982
> —*National Geographic*

They thought it dragged
its carapace like a steamer
trunk onto the highway, or slipped
out the gate someone left open,
disappearing like a sailing stone
into the lagoon. Years later, the father

passed, and the children
returned to rifle
his books, collectibles,
furniture, ephemera, yard
signs hoarded in the cellar. Imagine
the son struggling to grasp

raising and carrying a box
of vinyls to curbside, discovering what
he'd held as a child: the pattern
of scutes—dark at the margins,
muted inside, elephantine limbs
vivid with scales. Initially holed

up like a fossil, its neck
extended. Burrowed
in the rib cage, we humans
know we're a distrustful
kind. Or is it we surrender too

soon? What lives with us, in spite
of us? What
hides its methodology, slow
and steady, like a tortoise lapping
condensation in the shadow
of an *açaí* and feasting for three
decades on the plumpest raisins?

MEDITATION ON THE GREAT LAKE

She

spreads

out

her

threadbare

blanket

of

glass.

Purple.

Teal.

I

am

done

with

sad,

beige

girl.

O BODY OF BLISS

WHEN I CONTEMPLATE MY EXISTENCE

Alpacas, air, or anything earnest you are
bursting to say, bees, bees, bees, just being,
citrus everything, particular cypresses, Van Gogh's chair,
democracy, sliding doors, delight in others' delight,
elevator I used to fear, *swoosh* I didn't expect,
flash of minnow, the phantasmagoria of fish,
green landscapes under all that blue or the gilded
horns piped with pastry cream and hazelnut
inside their ruffled boats, the decked-out in
January, a snowperson juxtaposed—just
keeling over backwards, with the kneeling
little old man trying to repair, & I can't forget letting
Maddox bury his head in the dogfood bin, crunch machine;
next, all this color in the bend on River Trail North,
otter right there, & I'm like Odysseus saying odd
phrases to it, planning palinodes or the perfect
quote from a friend, getting myself quietly
ready in a room full of sunlight, & perhaps this recitation
seems radical, but somewhere, someone's studying
toddlers running or cell typology, a palm tucked
under the Earth, a rehabilitated animal, its unmistakable
voice like the end of a good book or the creak in a weather vane.
What if, what if, on an ordinary Wednesday,
X-shaped signs mean you belong, mark your X's,
your own list of greats, as if to say, you, now you:
zest.

SEX

At the table, I tell you
I walked toward it,

a current warm as broth.
about my childhood,

You,
I dove off summers

so long, I would
come, dressed

behind your future trees,
river, almost

downpour, champagne
taking what it wants.

sigh like wind, brush
and the summers

blossom not yet exploded,
on its knees, a bliss

for the next thing: a towel
verging on montage,

If Adam could,
pictures of Eve. Imagine

her foot that never quite
wanted heels to get lost

how the first time
the ocean kissed me,

You keep asking
but this is all:

the full-length deck like the one
as a girl, and my winters were

watch the snow
with sled and waiting. I hid

swam your future
became the shower:

spilling sugar,
In the dark, animals

windows with their tails,
burn to fall, one trumpet

the shrubbery
like God changing, searching

the color of Rome, a play
or the shy wheat in a field.

he would have taken
the arch of

touched ground. She
in the smell of moss

or to descend   stairs to cellars, hidden
skins of towns. In this,   I enter a museum back room,

rip off the wallpaper,   discover two paintings,
the sky and sun with   the plaza to themselves. You
take

my hand.   We move away from the table.
        Nervous,
the ceiling gathers stars from the sea. There's a boat. Water
                            with a private depth.
                            You carry me.

PRAYER FOR A STUDENT DRIVER

When you're out alone and trucks
surround like barricades, I hope the song
on the radio is that obscure
one that reminds you of when
the summer air was just
right. If you take a turn
down a zigzag road, I hope the fields

gift delicate beech, oak and fir
for deer to feed on, and let the squirrels
mid-street with their stop-start-stop have
rhythms like your own. When you're
lonely, notice the architecture of a lone
tree, the light hitting the canopy
until it bursts like that Fern

Hill green. Let the street be named Lovedale
or Lilypond or Via de la Vaille, and may it
bend as the hem of a dress, like a mother
who senses all you want is pocket change
and a key, a mother telling all the neighbors
how you traveled cross country, got a car,
a job out West, are into French cooking, found

love. May your life not be tragic or unkind; when
you leave as you must, let it
be the case you didn't hesitate
to say what you meant to the exact
person you meant to say it to. That at your exact
moment of departure, you crossed the seatbelt
over your chest until you felt, until you heard: *click*.

MEDITATION ON A LAVENDER FARM

My best friend lifts a wand,
wreath, chocolates, sixteen
sprigs, calls them *scented*

sins, and I can't wipe
the purple from her hair
when she says we could stand

to have a few more of them—
sins, that is. I need to sit
more before I commit to what I'll take

home. She doesn't know my
pride— not exactly showy,
emerges, a clean flush,

but wedges, broad as a small
plot, like a stone in my gut, or
that desire is sand, sinuous

in my hands. Oh, farmer whose
grandmother wanted
to be a farmer, but couldn't, can

you point and tell me how
to categorize based on gravity?
My car too

big—sin! I had a third
glass—sin! There
are mind altering drugs in my medicine

cabinet, and I've wanted more
time—sin! I've wanted
other men, not

including Blair Underwood and Javier
Bardem—not *No
Country for Old Men* Javier--

but *Eat, Pray, Love*,
the *Vicky Cristina
Barcelona* variation

on a theme of lavender,
a glass of Voignier
and Javier. Forgive

me, friend, this fragrant
land is both tenuous
and divine. Look

at us, risen,
descended, our limbs
walking right into where

the bees just
were, those pretty
little gods.

ON READING ESTHER PEREL'S
MATING IN CAPTIVITY

Your brows are two havens over
caves, and I imagine searching your sculpted

face as if reaching for
a handle of rock. I could swim

in your eyes' windows
abandoned homes. I know

that brunette hair means an entire
canopy of darkness, all

this moving through
midnight hours. Is it too

much to say *temperate*?
To say *glorious*

chest? There's no
ice here. I touch your

fingertip, trace all the way up your arm
to a small boulder. Have I ever

said your facial gestures are
elegant? Your belly moves

like an animal, like Monet's *Branch
of the Seine near Giverny*, and between

your legs: wildness,
forests, tropics.

AMONG THE THINGS SHE DOESN'T DESERVE
—after Dan Albergotti

Skillet potatoes with rosemary and shallots, a copper
bell's welcome ring, running the dog in a landscape
arboretum, hostas thick with smiles, fresh
eggs from a neighbor, a potted geranium, comfortable
transformation, oceanic
highway, the roasted note
of coffee houses, radish carpaccio like eight
amethyst moons, a seraphim angel's brown
hair and lifted eyelid
of night, an ease like a ball
kicked in the duomo square, the watchful
wall of cypresses, a moss
cashmere throw, a pat
on the back of a child, the peony
buds, the same air, the rain
chain filling, a tall
glass, the sky weeping snow.

AFTER THE MELT

February's known to kill, but this
morning, a light
vest for my run, the dog free

from his coat. It's time I brush
the leaves neglected
on the patio, sweep the sidewalk,

crack the windows, wipe the out
door table--it's warm enough
for a drink later if I ever

finish this run, Maddox sniffing
collapsed meringues of snow as if
he knows hope lives

in the seams of seasons. Today,
you've been gone three years,
and not that I take everything as a sign,

but the twelve geese
headed east, then
nine low to the west, then

four headed south, wasn't the story
of how when one's injured, another
from the flock stays

until it recovers or dies. The ground
has its own lacy openings
like latent grief I'm learning to

move with. Father, down a slope
of road I never go, a patch of green
bares itself. My dog likes to run

through with his thank you-thank-you-thank you
gait, and you'd want me to take an abrupt
change of course, because it's such a day,
and there's so much to do.

EVENING POEM TO BE READ TO A DOG

You who are descended from wolves, how
was breakfast with runny egg, your morning
run, the hoop you jumped, the couch's
islands of pillows, that shallow bowl

of water, crumb from last night's dinner, the stick
you flaunted, the toy you learned,
the ball from the bottom of the box, the sixth
nap? You who are miracle, you live unburdened

by reflection, though I never
agreed with Wittgenstein. You
anticipate my arrival. Let me sing of the colors;
you remind me of the brightness

I'm missing. You who are pure
absence of linguistic noise. Tomorrow, you'll wonder
where I've gone, so I promise to provide the effect
I am about; I'll play Monk or that Diane Lane/

John Cusak flick I watch too much. Faithful
companion, I curse that
someone somewhere abusing your kind. You,
high priest, lead me into the canyon where

I'll walk you through yellow
birch and black

ash. No awkward silence in your fixed
stare from the other

side of the living room that heard
me before I traipsed through the door.

IN THE WINTER OF MY SILENCE, THE ORACLE

speaks of patience in the face of what
keeps coming: the jab, the hook, the cross,
the uppercut, the reef
break, the beach break, the bump. The longest
record of consecutive days
without sun was fifteen in 1972.
Doesn't seem that bad
considering. Times, grace seems
stuck, delayed, no
unzipping her garment bag of light;
a stop off with no quiet path. Kids can sense
this, their expressions strained
or blank. Like metered tides or capes
untied, what comes together falls
away, pooled on the floor. Grief's
naked mostly to the self, the morning
sun trying to puncture the wall of clouds
like a fist.

WAYS TO HEAL A COUNTRY

Duct tape the hell out of it. Pour a plaster
mold. Let everyone sign. Take down
the drapes. Send out for cleaning or burn. Don't
have the people count off by twos. Light fifty
candles. Notice the glint in a brother's
eye as the sun's rays do their perfect
bounce, the atmosphere's atoms singing
a silent fireworks, an anthem
of remembrance. Repeat. Try
a woman. Dance with psychological
collapse, weep, chant, and wash your hands
raw. Rest the rivers. Ice
to reduce redness. Wrap
the mountains in fine
linen. To strengthen bone: broccoli,
oranges and papaya. Elevate
the children. Erase the demagogues'
complaints. Sip water clean as syntax.
Pocket a picture of an ancestor. Inscribe
grief on the back. Barter. Fry a sun fish. Put on
a recital. Let sympathy whorl
and trail like trillium. Brainstorm:
mend, amend, redress, restitution,
reparation. Say the word *we* 100 times followed
by *nuclear change*. Scoop a custard cool
as lake. Swim in it. Steep
tea with milkweed, native
wisteria and agarita. Label it *Spiritual
Awakening*. Seed

the feeders for the mourning
dove, cardinal, junco, and house
finch. Tend a community garden. Listen
with the frequency
of the greater wax moth. Rearrange
constellations. Make kirigami
from a CEO's quarterly reports or pages
of sacred texts. Print cards for an arts
education. Release the ultramarine
bowling ball of existential fear
from three fingers. Refrigerate the spray cheese.
Pack up the 30 aught six. Pick
up the peanut casings. Take
a bite of hotdog and go. See each
dead as your own.

O BODY OF BLISS

To friends abundant as red hair, to the rush
of cloud, sky and meadow, like calves
their first day on the grass. To the warm length
of a dog's back. To toast with butter
to feel how rich you are inside. To birth
marks and stretch marks. To the breath
like a stroll through a boxwood labyrinth.
To a pint cold in the hand. To oysters
giant as tears. To the edifice's moss.
To climb the Blue Ridge. To the smell
of sautéed turnips. To an almost oblique
sense of the hurt strewn your way, pours
on an encaustic painting. To the pomegranate's
sex and the sacred purpose of grapes. To
whatever bleeds on the lips. To the skin
from the sun. To the pill on the tongue.
To honey and Stilton. To the vein
they can never find; to the prayer forgotten.
To the bone healed, to the broken
fever. To morning. To the consciousness
of ocean and the reverence to good mothers.
To anything that flies. To ears for Miles
or Bach violin in E major. With every notch,
foramen, mandible and inlet, whatever it is
that moves you, you are moving toward flower,
toward the noiseless tint of sundown, a pulse
like a travel memory of what it was to walk here.

NOTES

The first opening epigraph is from Gaston Bachelard's book *The Poetics of Space* (Penguin Classics, 1958/1964).

The second opening epigraph is from Isak Dinesen's book *Seven Gothic Tales* (Reading Essentials, 1934).

"Walking Tour of Sacred Heart Cemetery:" Some of the information in this poem was taken from Monica Pryts' article "Stories Behind the Stones" in Grove City, PA's *Allied News* (Wednesday, September 2, 2020).

"Ode to the Airbnb:" "The house is in the body, the room is in us" are phrases in Gaston Bachelard's book *The Poetics of Space* (Penguin Classics, 1958/1964).

"When I Contemplate My Existence:" Some of the language in this poem was adapted from Elaine Scarry's *On Beauty and Being Just* (Gerald Duckworth and Company, 2006).

"Among the Things She Doesn't Deserve:" This poem is after Dan Albergotti's "Among the Things He Does Not Deserve" in *The Boatloads* (BOA Editions, 2008).

"Self-Portrait as a Hermit in the Wild:" Some of the language in this poem was adapted from Isabel Colegate's *A Pelican in the Wilderness: Hermits, Solitaries and Recluses* (Counterpoint, 2010).

"O Body of Bliss:" The concept "body of bliss" comes from Thich Nhat Hanh's book *The Heart of the Buddha's Teaching* (Harmony, 1999).

ABOUT THE AUTHOR

JANINE CERTO is the author of three full-length poetry collections: *O Body of Bliss* (2023), winner of the Longleaf Press Book Contest in Poetry; *Elixir*, winner of both the New American Poetry Prize and the Lauria/Frasca Poetry Prize (New American Press and Bordighera Press, 2021); and *In the Corner of the Living*, runner up for the Main Street Rag Poetry Book Award (2017). She is also the author of a poetry chapbook, *Home Altar*, winner of the Keystone Chapbook Prize (Seven Kitchens Press, forthcoming). A winner of the *Nimrod International Journal*'s Pablo Neruda Prize in Poetry, her poems appear in *The Cincinnati Review, The Greensboro Review, Poetry Northwest, Shenandoah,* and others. She is an associate professor at Michigan State University.

www.ingramcontent.com/pod-product-compliance
Lightning Source LLC
Chambersburg PA
CBHW022204090526
44583CB00012BA/478